The Whopper

The Whopper

"BB"

Illustrated by

D.J. Watkins Pitchford

MMXI • THE MEDLAR PRESS • ELLESMERE

Published by The Medlar Press Limited,
The Grange, Ellesmere, Shropshire.

ISBN 978-1-907110-21-4

*A limited edition of this book was published
by the Medlar Press in 1997.*

Typeset in 12 on 15 point Garamond Roman.
Produced in England by The Medlar Press Limited, Ellesmere, England.

Contents

"BB"

Denys James Watkins-Pitchford

Born Lamport, Northamptonshire 25th July 1905, died Sudborough 8th September 1990

Denys was brought up in comfortably Edwardian circumstances with his two brothers by their mother, Edith Elizabeth Wilson, and his father Walter, who was a vicar. Denys, thought to be 'delicate' as a child, was educated privately, which in his case really meant that, because he never went to school, being taught instead at home by a governess, his father and a local schoolmaster. His parents were musical, but emotionally distant and neither of them shared his love of the outdoors and so, constantly troubled by childhood illness, Denys lived in a small, almost hermetically sealed world which cast its eyes longingly back to another age; this had a profound effect on his character and his writing. His twin brother Roger, on the other hand, had a very different experience of life and was sent to boarding school, emigrating to Canada when he was in his early twenties.

Denys spent much of his spare time exploring the surrounding countryside, where he developed a tremendous love of nature as well as a passion for shooting and fishing. His parents were very class-conscious which, combined with the way he was educated, meant that he had little contact with other children and was taught to fish by local men like Job Perkins. Given his upbringing, it isn't surprising that Denys was socially awkward and he simultaneously valued and feared solitude; a contradiction which he spent a lifetime trying to resolve and accounted for his reserved character.

At fifteen, having failed to excel at anything in particular during his studies, Denys started a course at Northampton Art College, which came as a shock given his natural shyness, but although the course was very traditional, he developed an interest in scraper-board while he was there and managed to win a scholarship to Paris. In 1926, he went to the Royal College of Art, where he finally managed to get to grips with the world beyond the comforting fields of his home, although he still longed to return and he painted and drew birds and animals constantly in his spare time.

When he left the College in 1928, Watkins-Pitchford found himself at something of a loss about what to do, but after spending an entire summer fishing and shooting, he decided to become a schoolteacher. After weathering the General Strike, the grapevine brought him news of an assistant arts mastership at Rugby School, for which he successfully applied. Although teaching was hardly a vocation as far as Denys was concerned, it was an environment he understood and, when it boiled down to it, he was often more comfortable in the company of the boys than he was with adults, not that he would have volunteered for it. He stayed at Rugby for seventeen years, only leaving after the war's end.

Watkins-Pitchford started writing not long after he took up his post at the school, particularly for the *Shooting Times* - by then he had a fair amount of experience of goose shooting, in addition to his growing skill as a coarse fisherman. Then, in 1938, he had two manuscripts accepted (*The Sportsman's Bedside Book* and *Wild Lone, The Story of a Pytchley Fox*) and he began to appreciate that there might be a way to lead the life he had always dreamed about; so he set about writing with a will. He married Cecily Mary Adnitt in 1939, by whom he had a son, Robin and a daughter, Angela; sadly his son died aged only seven and his wife predeceased him by sixteen years.

In 1942, Watkins-Pitchford won the Carnegie medal for *Little Grey Men* and a light began to glimmer at the end of the tunnel; although he struggled to make ends meet until the end of the Sixties, an impressive stream of titles followed, at the rate of nearly one a year for the next three decades. He wrote all his books (apart from *Be Quiet and Go A-Angling*) under the pseudonym "BB", which was taken from a shotgun load used to bring down geese, and illustrated most of them using scraperboard, which prior to his use of the method had rarely been used outside advertising. He also contributed regular pieces to *The Field* and *Country Life*, becoming an icon of British sporting writing in the process, although this was only truly the case by the Eighties, by which time he was writing much less and was having regular haemodialysis.

"BB" wrote some fine fishing books, including *Be Quiet and Go A-Angling* (1949), *Wood Pool* (1958), and *The Whopper* (1967). *Be Quiet* was originally published using the pseudonym Michael Traherne, something "BB" later regretted and in 1987 he updated the book, published it under his own name "BB" and changed the title to *A Fisherman's Folly*. *Confessions of a Carp Fisher*, published in 1950, became a classic, partly for the quality of the writing, but also because it was the first book to identify carp fishers as a clan. When he wrote it, the record stood at twenty-six pounds; barely a year later, "BB" found himself sitting beside the carp lake at Woldale, in the company of his friends Richard Walker and Maurice Ingham, discussing why carp fishing wasn't more popular. From this conversation, the Carp Catchers' Club evolved. "BB"s involvement was ironic in a way, given that he fished for much the same reason that he shot - it was just a good excuse to be out enjoying the countryside. From that conversation, today's specimen carp fishing movement is descended and yet many of the people involved are unaware of the role "BB" played.

Andrew Herd

CHAPTER ONE

Tigger and Hoppy

Tigger Thomas was feeling bored as he wandered down the slope of the park.

There were crowds of people in the park and they all seemed to be enjoying themselves - all except Tigger. It was a lovely summer afternoon and everywhere he looked he could see grown-ups and children making the most of it.

But Tigger was feeling miserable because his mother had been called away that morning to her own mother who was ill up north in Warrington. His father was on night shift at the factory which meant that Tigger was all on his own and had to look after himself. During the day his father had to sleep so Tigger was learning to cook his own meals. As they had only recently moved to this town in the South Midlands, they did not know any of their neighbours.

Tigger was an independent lad. He enjoyed cooking his own meals, for now his father and he could have things which his mother refused to cook; things like tripe and onions, pig's head, and trotters. Although he missed his mother badly, he was enjoying his freedom, and having to look after himself for the first time made him feel he was a man.

Tigger, who was an only child, was tall for his age. He had carroty hair, a thin face and a lot of freckles on his nose. He wore a grubby T-shirt, blue jeans and sneakers. With his mother away, his clothes soon became dirty and he had decided not to try his hand at washing as well as cooking. He would manage without laundry work until she came back.

Really, Tigger had no excuse for being bored. This was the first day of the summer holidays and later in August his father and mother were taking him to the seaside. So he was luckier than many other boys of his age.

The big chestnut trees in the park cast pools of purple shadow on the grass where mothers with babies were sheltering from the hot sun.

Tigger strolled on down to the lake which was at the bottom of the sloping grass hill. There was an island in the middle of the lake which was not much bigger than a large pond.

On that hot afternoon the boating section of the lake was doing a roaring trade. All the tubby, brightly-painted boats were occupied by children who were propelling them around striving to ram each other.

As Tigger stood a moment, idly watching, one boat overturned, and the shrieking occupants were left standing up to their knees in water. Then a short man in a peaked cap, with a white terrier at his heels, emerged from a wooden hut near the boats and roared at them in a big stern voice. The squeals and shouts ceased at once. It was as though a flock of noisy birds had been frightened by a hawk.

Tigger had no intention of joining that unruly throng. His attention had been attracted by a small boy of about ten or eleven years of age sitting all by himself on the bank opposite the island. He had a rod in front of him, propped on a forked stick, and he was staring with deep concentration at a scarlet and white goose quill, which sat upright in the warm muddy-coloured water.

Tigger had no interest in fishing, in fact he regarded it as a kid's game. Cricket and football were more in his line, but something about the small vigilant figure attracted him. Tigger was a sociable character, and anyway, he wanted someone to talk to.

He came up and stood behind the boy, watching him silently. Why was it (he wondered) that fishermen never seemed to catch anything if you watched them?

"Any luck?" asked Tigger at length.

"Uh, huh."

Tigger took this to be 'yes'. He peered to see if there was anything in the glass jar which was half hidden in the grass by the angler's side, but there was nothing to be seen but misty water.

There followed another pause.

"I'm Tigger Thomas. My mum's gone to Warrington today to look after our gran, who's ill. That's why I've come to the park."

This information, given in a bright, amiable tone, failed to impress the fisherman. He remained staring at his float. Then he bent down and took a handful of small yellow objects out of a tin and flung them into the water around his float. They pattered down like rain.

"What's your name?" asked Tigger, who, besides being sociable, was very persistent.

"Any luck?" asked Tigger at length.

"Hoppy, Hoppy Doffton, and I've got no mum. Don't stand there, you'll scare the fish, and I'll never get a bite."

Tigger wondered why Hoppy hadn't got a mother, he thought everyone had a mother. This needed looking into. He sat down on the hot grass and examined his companion carefully. He noticed at once that Hoppy's left leg was encased in a sort of iron cage with straps round it, like the contraptions around the young newly-planted trees in the park.

He studied this for some time before continuing his examination of the grubby shorts and the dirty-grey flannel coat with a torn pocket. Hoppy's hair was mouse-coloured and had not felt a brush or comb, nor soap and water, for many a day. It protruded in every direction like a terrier's rough coat. The ears were enormous and stuck out like tea-pot handles, the nose turned up at the end, and the mouth was very wide.

Hoppy Doffton was certainly no beauty, yet Tigger decided he had a nice, honest, ugly face, humorous and tough. He liked it. He could be friends with this boy.

The examination over, Tigger said, without any beating about the bush,

"What you got your leg in that thing for?"

Hoppy still did not look round but kept his gaze fixed on his float, which was cocked, like a scarlet question mark, out in the thick warm water of the pond.

"Because it's not straight, that's why."

"Can't you walk proper? Can't you run like I can?"

"Course not, but I get along all right, nosey."

Tigger said nothing for a few minutes. Then he started his examination all over again, working down from the tousled head and big red ears, to the leg in its iron cage which seemed to fascinate him.

"Why isn't it straight?"

"Shut up, I've got a bite," snapped Hoppy, who was quite used to people remarking on his leg.

Tigger noticed that Hoppy's ears were twitching backwards which was rather surprising. It was a habit of Hoppy's with which Tigger was to become familiar. Hoppy always moved his ears when he was excited.

Tigger spent the next minute trying to move his own ears backwards, but they wouldn't stir. He let his gaze travel from his curious companion to the long glistening line which was tethered to the scarlet quill.

"Bah! Fishing is a mug's game, besides, there's only sticky-backs in here," observed Tigger with scorn.

The scarlet quill dipped and curtsied. Hoppy struck with a practised flick of his wrist. Out of the dun-coloured water came a skipping, jumping wisp of silver which Hoppy caught deftly with his outstretched left hand. He laid the rod down and with one gentle movement, unhooked the little fish, and dropped it into the jam-jar, which had a loop of string round the top to carry it by.

"There you are," said Tigger scornfully, "just what I told you, a stickyback!"

"Stickyback, my foot, it's a roach, a little one."

"Can I look?" asked Tigger crouching down by the jar, interested in spite of himself.

Hoppy didn't reply for he was busy rebaiting his hook with a wriggly grub which he extracted from a tin full of bran, which heaved and undulated as the maggots burrowed to get away from the light.

Tigger took up the jar carefully and held it close until his nose touched the cold glass. There was another little fish

Just opposite them was the island.

inside. It was different from the roach for it was a soft gold colour marked with bars, both had eyes like swivelling jewels. They darted about inside their glass prison with minute quivering fins.

"That other one's a stickyback, anyway," observed Tigger with confidence, anxious to air his knowledge.

"Never! It's a minnow."

Tigger remained silent, which was unusual for him when contradicted. Hoppy evidently knew what he was talking about and it wasn't any use arguing with him. Anybody could see he was an expert by the way he handled his tackle, he was no bent pin amateur.

Tigger sighed, then rolled on his side and propped his head on his hand, watching his friend with renewed interest.

The sun was very warm. The grass smelled of bleached hay. The shouts and cries of the children down by the boating pool at the far end of the lake sounded like the distant clamour of gulls, very sleep-making. Tigger let his eyes roam over the pond, drinking in all the details he hadn't noticed before.

In the industrial north, which had been his home since he was born, the green of summer was soon tarnished and worn. It was hard to breathe air which was not tainted. Yet he had made many friends there, and so had his parents. Though he had missed his old familiar streets and back alleys where he used to play, their new home had greater advantages. This smell of sun-bleached grass, for instance, was a real open air, country smell, and he liked it.

Just opposite them was the island on which grew dense shrubberies of box and holly, a few horse chestnuts, and one enormous black poplar shaped like an open fan. Tigger stared at its millions of leaves slightly shivering in the gentle summer breeze. It looked a very exciting island, full of mystery, even though it was not more than two hundred and fifty yards long by eighty broad. Two white swans stood on the bank preening themselves and rubbing the backs of their sinuous necks on their snowy white rumps.

Boats could be hired from the man in charge at a shilling an hour but nobody was allowed on the main lake. There was a floating wooden boom across from bank to bank and a large notice: No Boats Beyond The Barrier. Not even grown-up people were allowed on the main lake, which made the island all the more mysterious and unattainable. "What fun," thought Tigger, "if I could swim across when nobody was looking, and set foot on that forbidden shore!" He could swim well, he had learned in the public baths in Warrington, and being a bold lad, he could dive from the high board and had gained his life-saving certificate. Tigger's dreamy musings were rudely interrupted by an exclamation from Hoppy.

"Gosh!"

Tigger sat up. Hoppy was pointing out into the lake where he had thrown some small pieces of white bread from his lunch sandwich. A patch of water weed grew just opposite, with horizontal leaves shaped like the blades of Zulu spears. Among these weeds some large creature was stirring about. As Tigger stared an astonishing thing happened. There was a bulge under the weeds, and there appeared an enormous mouth, a hose pipe of a mouth. Behind it was a shiny head and an *eye*!

Tigger saw it quite distinctly. It was a most intelligent eye, which was looking, for a moment, on a totally different world of sun, blue sky, painted boats, and rustling trees. Tigger could have sworn that eye was looking directly at him with an expression of tremendous wisdom such as one sees in the eye of an elephant.

What made this apparition more startling and weird was a tendril of green water weed which was draped like a scarf over the glistening dome of its head. Then, as the boys watched, they saw a piece of bread twirl round like a scrap of soap in a plug hole. There was a loud smacking suck, a sluicing 'cloop',

and head and bread submerged. Ripples came furling to the bank. For a moment neither boy uttered a word, but Hoppy's ears were twitching backwards.

"Whatever was it, Hoppy, a Loch Ness Monster?" Tigger's eyes were bulging in astonishment.

Hoppy leant forwards and hastily wound in his line.

"So Tom was right," he said in a low voice, almost a whisper, "by Golly, Tom was right."

"Who's Tom?"

"Tom's the chap who looks after the boats, see. He's a friend of mine. Mostly he don't like small boys because they cheek him. I don't cheek Tom and he sometimes lets me have a boat for nothing. He told me last week there's a hell of a fish in here. He saw it one day, close to, sunning itself by the island, when he had to go out in the boat to fetch a kid's ball or something. Big as a hog, so Tom said, it quite scared him. He reckoned it must be a pike, but there's no pike in here, anyway. It hasn't got a pike's head. A pike's head is like a shovel."

Hoppy seemed a different character and was now quite talkative and full of animation.

"It's a carp, Tigger, that's what it is, and it's as big as I am. Record for this country is forty-four pounds, caught by a chap called Richard Walker, and he caught it at night. That's when the big fish feed, see. Reckon this fish is all of fifty pounds. Maybe nearer sixty. Gosh! Wouldn't I like to catch him!"

Hoppy's eyes were flashing, and his ears were twitching again.

"Cor! What a fish, Tigger. *What a fish!* Suppose we caught him. We'd be famous!"

"They'd probably give you a medal," Tigger said. All the same, Hoppy's excitement was catching.

Fishing wasn't a mug's game after all, this would be more like big game hunting!

"Suppose you hooked him, Hoppy, you'd never pull him out would you?"

"Just let me get him on," said Hoppy in a reverent voice. "I'll ask my Dad for a few tips and get him to lend me some tackle. This stuff is only for tiddlers, we'd need better line, bigger reel, and a big hook. I'd need a mighty lot of line. Fish like that would need a hell of a lot.

"This hot weather is just right for carp, see. They always bite best when the water's warm. What are you doing tomorrow morning, Tigger, real early I mean? About five o'clock say. How are you fixed?"

"You bet I'll come!" exclaimed Tigger. "Dad's on night shift and won't be home till nine, and I've nothing to do."

Hoppy dropped his two little fishes back into the lake. A wrinkle on the surface, and they were gone. He pulled his rod apart and put it carefully into his bag.

"See you tomorrow then, I'll meet you here." "OK Hoppy, I'll be here!"

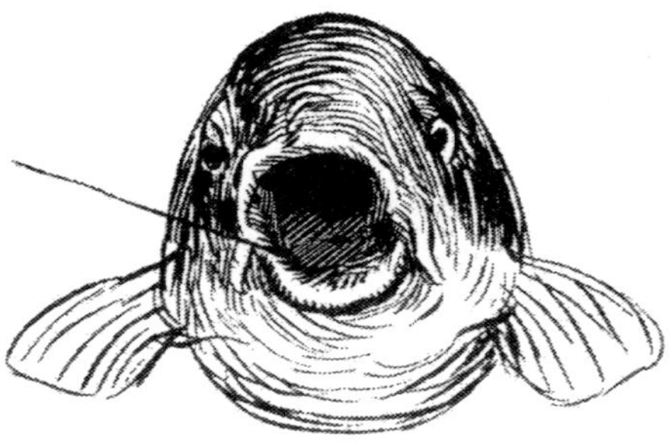

CHAPTER TWO

Dawn Escapade

Tigger found it hard to get to sleep that night. He kept on seeing that monstrous head and eye emerging from the water. Somehow he had a vague feeling he had seen something like it before. Then he remembered. There had been a reproduction of a richly-coloured painting on the classroom wall at school. It was by a Flemish artist called Hieronymus Bosch. It was a picture full of the strangest creatures, pots and pans with legs, some half-animal, half-human, and in one corner was a monstrous fish emerging with a funnel-shaped mouth, and the legs of a man were disappearing down it. He had often examined that painting with fascination and wonder.

When at last he fell asleep, he saw that mouth again. It was such a nightmare he was glad to wake. The light of dawn was already in his room, dim and grey. A blackbird was warbling from the plum tree in their strip of back garden. For one dreadful moment he thought that he had overslept, but as he dressed he heard the reassuring clock of St Michaels and All Angels strike four. He boiled himself an egg, and ate a slice or two of the cold bacon Mum had left for her menfolk to 'cut at' whilst she was away.

Then he slipped out of the house. The sweetness of early morning air was something new to Tigger. He took deep breaths as he hurried along the deserted pavements, where home-going cats trotted and stopped with uplifted delicate paw and suspicious gaze.

It was a good twenty minutes' walk to the park. The dew wet his shoes as he ran down over the grass to the lake. Blackbirds were warbling at one another from the green chestnuts, whose leaves were unstirring in this curiously changed world of quiet. Already among the splayed leaves conkers were forming, to be gathered later in the year on golden October afternoons as children came home from school. A thin veil of mist cloaked the lake and island. Tigger could see the fan-shaped top of the black poplar showing above it. It seemed magically suspended in mid-air, like a mirage. Through the gossamer veil of ground mist a small hobbling figure materialised, burdened with a large rod bag, enormous net, and a bait can. Hoppy grinned a wide grin.

"You've made it then, Tigger. I thought somehow you would. It's a smashin' morning for fishing!"

The two boys hurried eagerly down the slope, their shoes black with the dew, until they reached their pitch opposite the island.

The whole place seemed quite different from daytime. At the far end the painted boats were drawn up neatly in a row, silent and waiting. Some wild duck were swimming about, but took quacking wing when they saw the boys. Not another living person was in sight.

From one end of the island a long-legged, long-necked bird sprang into the air and went fogging away with wide cup-shaped wings.

"Coo! There goes a stork!" exclaimed Tigger, catching at Hoppy's sleeve.

"You've got a lot to learn, Tigger. That's no stork, it's a heron. They only come here when nobody's about. Now don't make no noise, Tigger," Hoppy lowered his voice, "and don't go trampin' about on the grass. Fish can see and hear us, least-ways, they can feel vibrations like."

Hoppy drew out his rod from the bag, which was carefully tied with tapes. It was much larger than the one he had used the day before, so was the centre-pin Nottingham reel, made of wood.

"My Dad's pikin' reel," whispered Hoppy, as he carefully threaded the line through the rod rings.

"I've got over a hundred yards of line here, ten pound breaking strain and all."

To Tigger's surprise Hoppy tied the large number two hook direct to the end of the line without float or sinker. He pulled off at least a dozen yards from the reel and greased it from a little tin, between thumb and first finger.

"That's to make it float, see," whispered Hoppy.

He pinched out a lump of white bread flake from the centre of a small loaf and buried the sharp barb in it. He took off his coat and spread it, inside uppermost, on the grass, and coiled his line on it so that it would not catch on the grass blades.

Holding the line just above the reel in his left hand he

swung the bread out and dipped it once in the water to give it weight. Then with one steady underarm swing he sent it flying outwards, the line flickering off the coat spread on the grass. As the bread curved downwards at the end of the throw Hoppy lowered the rod point, and it plopped neatly into the pond some sixty yards short of the island.

"Coo! that's a good cast!" exclaimed Tigger.

Hoppy now stuck a forked stick among the rushes in front of him and rested the long slender rod gently in it, coiling some ten feet of line on the bank. The two boys settled down to wait. The grass was still wet so they sat on their coats. As they watched the floating flake, they spoke in whispers as though they were in church.

Tigger found he was not at all bored, there was so much going on, birds active in the park trees, a moorhen and her sooty chicks pecking about among the waterlily leaves, and ducks splashing about by the boating pool.

Now and again the floating flake was pushed about and butted by small rudd and roach, but there was no sign of the big carp. Tigger wondered where it was, what it was doing. Questing about among the reeds no doubt, its cunning little eyes swivelling to and fro, searching for some morsel, quite unaware that two small boys were planning its downfall!

Hoppy's eyes were fixed on the floating flake. He was oblivious to anything else. Whenever the bread showed movement his ears twitched. He reminded Tigger of an alert terrier watching by a rat hole. Now that he came to think of it, Hoppy was *very* like a tough little terrier! He had the same tenacity of purpose and powers of concentration, the same rough hair!

Minute by minute now the scene was changing and much

of the magic of the dawn world was draining away. They could hear the traffic beginning to rumble on the main road at the far side of the park, and factory hooters going. A few people, night workers going home, were now walking across the grass. The sun came up over the willows by the boating pool. The muddy-coloured water began to steam gently in the warm rays.

"I'm going to have breakfast," announced Hoppy in a low voice, pulling a packet of sandwiches from his pocket. "You've had yours, so watch that bread. It's just when the sun gets on the water that he's likely to get on the move. Tom'll be here soon, and the kids will be arriving so we might as well pack up then. O hell! Here come the flippin' swans!"

The two proud white birds came sailing round the corner of the island and bore down upon Hoppy's line. They surged onward in jerks, propelled by their muscular black paddles with a hump of water at each snowy breast and a furling wake behind.

"I'll soon settle them."

Hoppy took a catapult from his pocket and putting a lead shot in the leather pouch, let fly. The water splashed in front of the leading bird. He swung about. Hoppy had hardly sat down when, from out of the dark band of water by the island, arose the wondrous fish. It did not come clear out of the pond for its weight was too great. It heaved itself upwards and swooned back with a mighty splash that sent ripples furling across to them.

"Gosh!" exclaimed both boys together. "Gosh!"

"What did I tell you?" said a gruff voice behind them which made them jump. "I knew you thought I was telling you a tale when I said there was a monster in here. But don't let me catch you stoning them swans, Hoppy, or you'll not come fishing here any more."

It was Tom the boatman. He had a pipe in his mouth and his little terrier, Skipper, was at his heels.

The boys had been so excited watching the fish they had not heard him approach.

"That's his favourite swim," went on Tom, "I often see him jump there in the mornings. It's deepish water all round the island, see, and I reckon he lives there, plenty of grubs falling off the trees. You keep pegging away Hoppy. You'll very like get him one of these days. There was a lad fishin' where you are, a year ago, and I reckon he hooked him. I was passing at the time and his rod went like a matchstick. If some of the local angling lads knew there was a fish like that in this little pond we'd have them all here! But I reckon he's cunning. He must have been in here years to grow to that size. I've seen no others like him. All the other fish are little ones. You've never seen that fish Hoppy, not the whole of it. I saw it last winter when the pond was frozen over. I was on the island seeing the kids didn't damage the bushes and that. The ice was clear, clear as glass, and I happened to look down and see him lying doggo on the bottom. Regular pickle barrel, he was, fat as a pig."

"What weight would he be, Tom?" asked Hoppy.

"Near sixty I reckon. Not far off it any road. Well, must be getting along, the kids are coming. Remember about the swans, Hoppy. No more stoning, or you won't come any more."

Tom stumped away towards his hut leaving behind him a fragrant cloud of shag tobacco. When he had gone, the boys sat watching the dark channel opposite. Twice a great tail came up and waved like a flag.

It was Tom the boatman.

"That's him, standing on his nose," whispered Hoppy. "Greedy old Pickle Barrel. He's eating little blood worms or something on the bottom, see. Tom's right, you know, that's his favourite swim. But it's no use. We can't reach him from here, not even with a fixed-spool reel, and I'd never do it with this centre-pin."

"I'll chuck a bit of crust out," suggested Tigger, "I'm a good chucker."

Hoppy shook his head. "You'd never reach it, not by throwing. I've got a better idea, though. You see Tom ain't looking. I'll put a crust over with my catty. "

Hoppy drew his catapult from his pocket, and hiding a lead sinker in the middle of the bread and pinching the flake round it, he put it in the leather pouch and pulled. The bread landed slap in the middle of the channel. To the boy's astonishment there was a swirl almost at once. The white crust was sucked under.

"There you are!" exclaimed Hoppy excitedly. "See that? Took it like a lamb. He'd never suspect anyone could reach him there, see?"

Hoppy's ears were twitching, there was a wicked look in his eye. "Tell you what, Tigger, we've got to get over to that island."

"How? Nobody's allowed there! Would Tom put us over?"

"Tom! Not on your life! More than his job's worth. No! We've got to build a raft Tigger. We've got to get over at night. Game for a try?"

"You bet!" Tigger exclaimed. "When shall we start?"

CHAPTER THREE

The Raft

Hoppy Doffton's father was a scrap-iron merchant and they lived in Eden Street. He also dealt in other things as well, odds and ends which people were only too glad to get rid of when they were moving house. So he managed to get all sorts of rubbish cheap. Tigger found the Dofftons' yard a truly fascinating place when he visited it later with Hoppy.

"Dad's out with the lorry," his friend explained as he conducted him round the premises. "I don't see much of him, not week days, as he's not home till evening, and then he often goes to the pub with his pals. At weekends he's off with the club, fishing, and if I catch him in a good mood I go with him, but the other members aren't keen on kids going along. I'm not worried, though. I spends all my spare time fishing, and Dad don't mind where I go, or how long I stay out, as long as he knows where I'm going. Sometimes a neighbour comes and cooks a bit of grub for us, and cleans up, like, and does the washing, but Dad's not too keen on the neighbours poking their noses in, so we more or less manage for ourselves. When I'm older, Dad says I'll be a partner in the business, and go round with him in the lorry. He's a good sort is Dad. He'd be thrilled if we caught that record carp, I can tell you."

While Hoppy was talking, Tigger let his gaze roam over the extraordinary collection of objects which were stacked on all sides, leaving only enough room for Mr Doffton's lorry, where there was an oily, greasy patch with tyre marks.

There were old boilers, rusty, tyreless bicycles, brass bedsteads, broken kitchen chairs, refrigerators, old street lamp standards, TV sets, a leather armchair with horse hair stuffing protruding, sofas, old lavatory pans and cisterns, ball-cocks, iron pipes, paving stones, two striped mattresses, (a mouse's nest was in one of them with no extra charge), 'Tortoise' type heating stoves and rusty chimneys, a barrow without a wheel, a rusty Triumph motorcycle 1920 vintage, without any tyres (Tigger got astride this and made a revving noise), a white bath, complete with taps, and piles of old red 'Shell' petrol cans, and jerricans, ex-USA army type.

At one end of the yard was a workshop. Its roof was of corrugated iron full of holes, but inside Tigger found it was fitted up with a workbench, a vice, and many tools, carefully hung on nails along the walls.

"Reckon we can rustle up something out of this lot," said Hoppy waving his hand airily over the junk yard, "Dad won't miss a thing, and anyway he likes me to be occupied."

"How about that old hip bath," suggested Tigger indicating a chipped brown and white affair up in one corner, "wouldn't that float?"

"Full of holes," said Hoppy, "and anyway it's too cranky."

Clambering over the junk.

"What about that old door?"

"Good idea, let's drag it out."

But it was terribly heavy, solid oak with iron hinges. They could hardly lift it.

"I know!" exclaimed Hoppy. "Just got an idea."

He went into the corner of the shed where large sheets of plaster-board and a ladder were propped against the wall. He disappeared behind these (no easy matter for him, clambering over the junk with his leg iron) and rummaged about like a big rat behind the boards.

"What a tough little customer he is," thought Tigger, "he always seems to have some job on hand."

It had been a bit of luck meeting him in the park. He could see there would never be a dull day now with nothing to do. Hoppy was pretty smart, too, at his lessons. He had casually mentioned that next term he was going to the Grammar School in Park Avenue, so he must be pretty brainy.

Tigger was a hopeless duffer at his own school and was always bottom of his class. "Never mind, we can't all be clever," thought Tigger. Perhaps, with Hoppy, his brains made up for the ailing leg, though it had to be admitted that Hoppy seemed to get along almost as well as he could.

"Come on, give us a hand!" A muffled voice came from behind the plaster-board.

Tigger negotiated the tangle of pipes, planks, and boxes, making a far greater business of it than Hoppy, and at last reached his friend.

"Catch hold and pull," Hoppy said. "This thing is jammed."

The 'thing' turned out to be the runner of what looked like a sledge. They hauled and struggled for all they were worth.

One of the big boards fell down in a cloud of dust and Tigger landed on his back with one foot in a tea chest.

When at last they dragged the object into the yard, Tigger saw it was a wooden sledge with wide wooden runners, the sort that polar explorers used with dog teams. They heaved it upside down, runners uppermost.

"That won't float," said Tigger, "not with that slatted seat. Leastways it won't with us on it."

"It won't take two anyway," said Hoppy, "but it'll take us one at a time. You'll soon see what I have in mind."

He led the way to a pile of empty petrol tins and handed two to Tigger. "We'll make sure there's no holes in them. Take yours to the tap, over there by the shed, you'll find a hose on it. I'll bring some more. We'll need six aside."

They stacked the twelve cans by the water tap and shook them upside down. Rust and spiders fell out, but all the cans, except one, were sound, and that was quickly replaced. They saw that each cap fitted tightly. Then Hoppy fetched some stout six-inch nails from the workshop. He hammered these in all round the wooden sides of the sledge and placed the cans in position on the underside, six down each side, between the runners. With stout wire and pliers he wired them tightly to the bottom of the sledge and made sure all were firm and immovable.

"They'll act as floats, see?" said Hoppy, standing back at last and surveying their handiwork, "and now we'll find a carriage for it."

From another pile of rubbish in the corner Hoppy pulled out the chassis of a pram. Upon this he placed the sledge, cans uppermost, and secured it tightly with stout rope.

An old cricket bat was produced from the back of the work-

The pram wheels wheezed and squeaked.

shop bench. Hoppy put it in the vice and planed some of the wood off the back to make it lighter.

"Jolly good paddle," said Tigger admiringly when he had finished, "but won't we need two?"

"One's enough," Hoppy said, "we shan't have any rowlocks, and we shall have to go over one at a time." He fetched a coil of cord, and drove a staple in one end of the sledge, and coiled the line on top of the cans.

"That's our tow line, see. You'll go over first Tigger, paying out the line as you go, see, and then when you're over, I'll pull it back and come over myself. Let's have a trial run down the road, we want to see how she travels."

The boys pulled the contraption out of the yard and took it down as far as the corner of Eden Street. It travelled well, though the pram wheels wheezed and squeaked, a fault which was rapidly cured by a squirt from an oil can.

"Now," said Hoppy, when they had returned to the yard, "you go home and have your tea. I'll square Dad when he comes in. He said himself that our only chance to catch Pickle Barrel is at night."

"What time shall we start?" asked Tigger, fairly dancing with excitement.

"Make it late, real late, about half-past midnight. We should be down by the lake by one or earlier. We'll both get over to the island and fish till six, see. Then we'll have to pack up and get away before Tom comes to the boats. If we don't catch Pickle Barrel tonight - tomorrow I mean - then we'll go each night until we do catch him."

"Half-past twelve then," said Tigger excitedly, "at the corner of the street, OK?"

"OK."

OFFTON

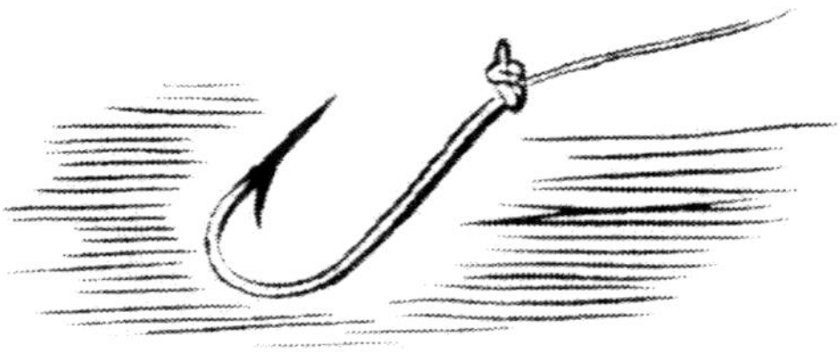

CHAPTER FOUR

The Castaway

Tigger reached Eden Street that night without meeting anyone, not even a policeman. He found Hoppy waiting for him with the loaded truck; upon it was his rod, tackle, large landing net, a can with a wire handle, full of bread, and a bag of provisions.

On their way to the park they met only two people, a home-going young couple walking arm in arm, who were far too interested in each other to notice the boys.

It was quite hard work pulling the load, and harder still when they left the road and went down over the grass of the park, for the narrow pram wheels bit into the turf. Soon they could see the lake in its hollow, as black as ebony, reflecting the quiet stars and a quarter moon which lit the summer night with magic. Tigger felt a tingle of excitement.

They worked in silence unloading the truck, pausing now and again to see if the coast was clear. At last all was ready for the dramatic moment. The raft was pushed into the water. Tigger scrambled aboard. They were delighted to find the sledge floated beautifully on the cans, just as Hoppy had said it would, the water just lapped the slatted seat. As Tigger pushed off with his paddle there was a most exciting scent of crushed water mint and pond water, it almost *smelt* of Pickle Barrel.

"Don't forget to pay out the line," whispered Hoppy, giving a final shove, "and when you get ashore, give a whistle and I'll pull her back."

Tigger nodded. He put his hand in the water; it felt quite warm, warmer than his fingers. He grasped the paddle by the handle and started off. The craft revolved as he went along. He found he had to row first on one side then on the other, and the paddle left behind little spinning water whorls at each stroke. It was a most exciting journey. It seemed to take a long time to reach the dark shadows of the trees where the chestnuts hung right over the water. They appeared to be swimming towards him. The only sound was a secret gurgle and cluck of water under the cans. Hoppy was holding the other end of the line and it paid off over the stern without a hitch.

Gently the raft bumped on the magic shore. Tigger jumped on to the ivy. What a moment! Here he was, safe and sound on the forbidden ground! Now Pickle Barrel was surely in for a big surprise! Tigger unloaded the rod, net, bait can, and bag of food. He placed the paddle on top of the raft and was just about to give the signal for Hoppy to pull on the line when, to his astonishment, he saw him pushing the pram chassis into the water. He seemed in a great hurry over it, stumbling and heaving. Then he waved frantically at Tigger, turned about, and hobbled away up the park as fast as he could go!

Tigger stood astounded. He dare not call out. Whatever was the matter?

Then he saw the reason for the hurried departure. A dark figure was sauntering down through the trees, a tall dark figure, crowned by a domed helmet. A policeman! Poor Hoppy with his stumbling gait could not make fast going, and to Tigger's horror, he saw the Bobby set off in pursuit, walking quickly with long strides. Then the shadows hid them from view.

A dark figure was sauntering down.

Unknown to the boys there had been some damage done to the boats by vandals the night before and Tom had told the police.

What was he to do; stay on the island and carry on fishing, hoping that Hoppy would return? Or should he embark again, make for the bank, and get away unseen? He was tempted to make a run for it.

He stood irresolute under the dark trees, pondering. Then he decided. Stay of course! Now he was here it would be stupid not to have a go at catching the giant fish. Hoppy had shown him how to cast and how to tie on the hook with a special fisherman's knot, which he'd been practising all the evening. The tackle was all there with the rod. The reel, line, and hooks were in the tackle bag, tucked in with the bait. Why not?

It was very ghostly on the island. The bushes were so thick and the trees overhead shut out so much of the faint moonlight he seemed to be in a gloomy cave.

He decided to explore before beginning operations. He pushed through the bushes, startling sleeping birds. A rat scuttled away. Then the bushes thinned. He found himself in a small clearing. In front of him was a tumble-down wooden hut affair, evidently the swans' hut, for white feathers glimmered in the dusk. The swans were absent, up by the boat pool, sleeping with their long necks on their backs. They preferred the open water to the rat-infested island. The doorway of the hut was like a black hole, it looked creepy.

Tigger pushed back through the bushes to where he had left the gear and the raft. He put the rod and tackle at the foot of the big poplar, where he could find them in the dark, and, with some effort, hauled the raft up on the bank until the

It was very ghostly on the island.

bushes screened it from anyone on the opposite shore. The policeman might return.

Then he began to tackle up, no easy matter in that bad light. They had forgotten to bring a torch, a bad mistake. But he managed. He threaded the line, by feel, through the rod rings, and tied the hook securely on to the end, holding it up against the dim moonlit sky. It was no trouble to cast out, he had only to swing the flake outwards like a pendulum and let it plop into the black water not ten feet away, right in the centre of Pickle Barrel's swim! Then he settled down to wait, making sure that he had coiled enough free line from the reel in case the great fish went off with his bait and felt a suspicious check. Hoppy had been very insistent on this.

This strange dead world, where nothing seemed to be moving, and all was so still, was most unnerving to a city-bred boy. This was quite a different matter to the dawn fishing. Then, birds sang and the light was growing all the time, things were waking up. Now, people had crept to bed like fowls to roost, even the rumble of traffic on the far side of the park was stilled. For a moment he had a sense of panic, and he had to take hold of himself. All about him was the wild tang of the pond water and hardly a sound save the splash of a fish out in the lake, or furtive rustle of a rat in the undergrowth behind him. A water vole swam across, looking like a blunt-nosed tug. It left a V-shaped ripple which rocked the scraps of ground bait Tigger had thrown around his flake.

Soon a young tawny owl came to the black poplar above him. It was hungry. Every four seconds, as regular as a clock, it gave its plaintive hunger cry, 'kee-weeet kee-weeet'. Then silently, its mother arrived like a winged shadow, and they both flew away together in the ghostly moonlight to the far mounds of chestnut.

Tigger was glad when it went, but for some time he still heard it, far away now, up the park, and the sound seemed to intensify his loneliness.

These country night noises in the centre of a large town showed that even amongst pavements, houses, bricks and mortar, nature was never far away and was ready to take over when mankind slept.

Tigger began to feel hungry. He took a sandwich from the bag and munched it as he watched the glimmering scrap of bread. What had happened to Hoppy? Had the policeman caught him? Hoppy would no doubt spin a very plausible tale, but it was strange he had not come back.

He heard the clock of St Michael's church strike two over the sleeping town. Everything had fallen very still now, not a rustle nor a splash, no owl crying. He began to feel sleepy. He propped himself against the black poplar and shivered. If Hoppy hadn't come back by five o'clock he'd pack it in, ferry back to the shore, and try to get the raft on to the pram chassis, though it would be a job to manage on his own. He hoped that Hoppy hadn't sunk it in deep water. No! On second thoughts perhaps it would be better to swim to the bank, leaving the boat on the island. He could swim six times this distance from bank to shore, though he'd have to look out for weeds. A moorhen 'cruiked'. Then silence again. A glow over the town. No sound of traffic. What about a nap?

Forty-four years before, on another June day in 1922, a small boy, known to his boon companions as Whiff Evans, had captured Pickle Barrel from the mill pool at Town Meadow. The fish could have hardly been called a Pickle

Barrel then, for he was little bigger than a pepper-pot and much more chubby, in fact he was no more than three and a half inches long, and looked like a bronze goldfish, to which family he belonged. He was then exactly a year old and weighed only a few ounces.

With great satisfaction Whiff had put him into his seaside bucket which had pink crabs, white sails, and blue seas painted on the sides. The infant Pickle Barrel jumped out twice on the way home and flipped about the dusty pavement until he was grabbed and returned to six inches of muddy river water. When Whiff had reached home his mother had said, "I'm having no fish in my house, with you slopping about with water. Give it to the cat."

Whiff thought otherwise. He had taken a fancy to his chubby little captive and he bothered to walk a mile to the park where he released Pickle Barrel by the boat station.

Whiff Evans was killed in the second world war so Pickle Barrel had survived him. Incredibly he had survived many narrow escapes in the Park Pond.

Once a heron stabbed at him and missed by a scales' breadth, which was unusual, for the heron was experienced and skilful with his fish spear. He had been hunted by otters many times, for otters are great travellers by night, even in populated areas, as well as clever fisher-animals. There had also been narrow squeaks, in his early uneducated years, from appetising worms, grubs, and lumps of dough, which were attached to hooks, hooks which were attached to lines, and the lines to small hopeful boys on the bank. Because of his strength, for he was growing fast, he broke free.

Boys' tackle is nearly always too frail, nets are hardly ever carried, and carp are doughty fighters. His latest escape had

Whiff had put him into his seaside bucket.

been the previous summer when, in an unguarded moment, he had scoffed a wriggling worm near the bank. Of course he had snapped the tackle in a moment and left a small boy with a broken rod and in floods of tears, and Tom, the boatman, full of wonder.

In the pond Pickle Barrel found abundance of food, for it was not overstocked with fish. There were no other carp for company, only roach and rudd. His diet was varied. In the summer-time there were grubs and caterpillars which dropped off the island trees, little floating flies, small blood worms, and transparent slugs which harboured on the undersides of the water-lily leaves. He loved to bask on hot days under these flat leaves which were like sunshades. He would lie for an hour or more, like a great blue-grey airship, occasionally stirring a lazy fin or giving a slight wag to the tips of his tail.

Small girls and old ladies fed the ducks with bread. This formed another item in his diet, though he only scoffed the floating pieces which had escaped the ducks and had drifted before the winds to the island where he loved best to lie.

When the sun of June brought a green fire to the overhanging chestnut leaves, Pickle Barrel would feel pleased with life, and, perhaps longing for a lady carp, he would throw himself, like a salmon, into the air (though in these later years his weight was so great he could only get his head and shoulders out, and sink backwards into the pond).

Then, when winter came, and the surface of the lake became one thin, grey, elastic sheet of ice, he would hear the singing of skates and feel the massive ceiling above his head sway and crack from shore to shore with sounds like pistol shots. But Pickle Barrel did not heed these disturbances. He was safe from hunting otters and scheming fishermen, both feathered and human, so he dreamed his own dreams down in his soft clay bed.

Suddenly Tigger was very wide awake. From along the bank on his right came a giant's gulp. Ripples came wheeling outwards. He had the eerie feeling that some enormous underwater monster was advancing stealthily on his bait. Tigger felt the small hairs on his scalp creep and stand up like the fur rises on the back of an angry dog. As he peered out across the dark, troubled water he felt his heart thump. Alone on the island, he had a sudden fear that he was about to be sucked into the depths of a gigantic mouth.

Fascinated, he saw his motionless white flake glimmering on the black water. As he watched it, it began to twirl.

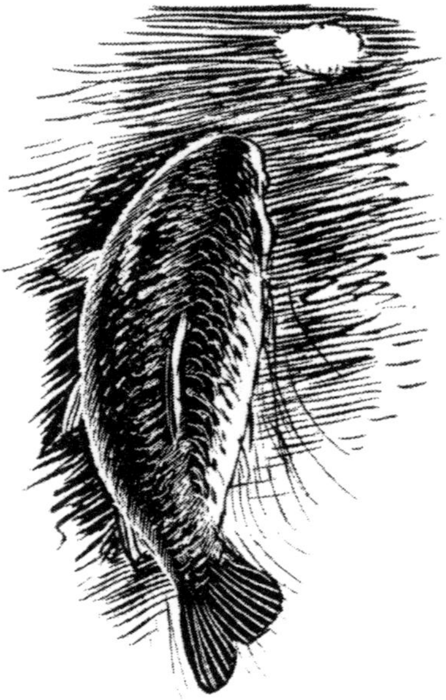

Then it disappeared. His finger came to life and went down the coiled line. It was whispering out into the darkness of the pond!

Then warmth returned to his startled body and excitement sped, like the agitated line, up and down his spine.

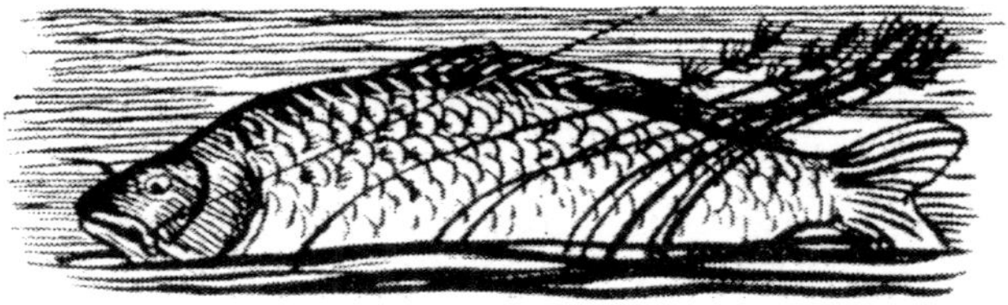

CHAPTER FIVE

The Long Night

Tigger waited, trembling, until all the line had whispered away. He made sure the check was on the reel. (If only Hoppy could see him now!)

Now for it! Then, he took up the rod butt. With his right hand on the cork, and his left up the rod, he struck with all his force. It was like hitting a sand bag. The rod bent dangerously. At once he felt an unbelievable pressure on the line. Things became confused. Something like a submarine shot outwards into the lake with a furl of water on either side, even the cork rod handle bent with the pressure.

Some years earlier Tigger had had a craze for kite flying, and once when a gale blew up, and whirled his kite high over the chimney pots, he felt as though he was fighting a giant. Then the string had broken and he saw his kite waver downwards a mile away behind some factory chimneys.

He had the same feeling now. He was attached to some

huge underwater creature of great strength and his line threatened to part at any moment.

The rod point bowed and bowed until it almost touched the water; he just couldn't hold that fish. In one blind rush it had taken fifty yards of line at least and was still travelling, the reel check screaming. It made such a dreadful noise in the silence of the night it must have been audible from the road at the top of the park.

"I'll never get him," whimpered Tigger aloud. "He'll break me, I can't hold him! I wish Hoppy was here!"

When Tigger felt that thrilling pull at the end of the line, he felt as if he had experienced all this before. It was lucky for him that he had tied the hook securely with the fisherman's knot which Hoppy had shown him; it was lucky for him that he had on his reel over one hundred yards of line; line tested to a breaking strain of ten pounds dead weight. It was lucky for him that he had the check on the reel and that it did not jam or over-run - which centre-pin reels are likely to do in inexperienced hands. But the greatest luck of all was that, when he had hit the fish, he had driven the number two forged steel hook right up beyond its wicked barb and that it was now buried in the gristly corner of Pickle Barrel's leathery mouth.

At the end of his charge the fish went deep down in the mud, somewhere between Tigger and the boating pool, eighty yards away. He stood on his big nose. He threshed the line with his broad lobed tail which served him as propellers, like those of a ship. They were his main engines, though he also had his spoon-shaped pectoral fins which helped in propulsion, but were mostly used, like his back fin, for altering direction. But that great tail, with its two sensitive lobes, could

drive him through the pond at a remarkable rate, certainly faster than Tigger could run on land.

"If he takes any more line, he'll break me," moaned Tigger in torment. The line was humming like a harp string. He could feel the vibrations as Pickle Barrel's tail struck. What he was really doing was to bury himself head first in the mud. To do this he used his main engines. He was not hitting the line to break it, he hadn't the sense for that.

Pickle Barrel's forty-five-year-old fish brain told him to get right under the mud; Tigger's superior twelve-year-old brain said, 'get along the bank before he makes another rush'.

This wasn't easy. Bushes, nettles, and reeds grew on the island verge. The reeds had edges which cut like razors. But this was no time for shirking. Tigger edged along, one foot in the water, one on the bank. Once he stumbled into a deep hole which wet him to the waist, but he saved himself by a frantic grab at a willow branch. In this way, stumbling desperately along in the dark, Tigger gained some thirty yards, until he found himself opposite the boat station.

In his first fear-crazed rush Pickle Barrel had made for a bed of water-daisy which grew just there, and if he had gone into it things would have been tricky for Tigger. But the side strain from the line had turned him and now he was burrowing in the clay, sending up clouds of mud, which billowed upwards.

Tigger could see a mass of needling bubbles exactly over Pickle Barrel's resting place.

"I must keep the line taut like Hoppy told me," thought Tigger, "Oh! How I wish he was here." Pickle Barrel then ceased to beat the line with his tail. He lay quite still, wondering what to do next, and why his head was being pulled on one side. Tigger was also wondering what to do next. It was fish brain against boy brain. Both had advantages.

Now the line began to travel again. Tigger had to begin winding in to keep the line taut. Pickle Barrel was coming in towards the island. "Now, if he goes right round the island, I've had it," thought Tigger. The pace became faster. Now the line was cutting a feather in the water as the fish increased speed.

"No you don't my lad," said Tigger out loud, pulling the rod point sideways to try and hold the fish from making a sweep right round the corner. The pressure made Pickle Barrel change his mind.

He found it most unpleasant driving forwards with his head pulled continually to one side. He changed tactics, he turned about and charged in towards Tigger's feet. The line went slack. Tigger thought he'd lost him. He reeled in frantically, as fast as he could turn the handle. On his left a willow bush grew half in the water. If the fish elected to go round that he'd have to follow.

Pickle Barrel not only went round the bush, he drove *through* the slender, whippy willow boughs which went under the surface at that point. This bush was a favourite haunt of his. On hot days he liked to rub his scales against the twigs, much as a cow rubs itself on a fence post. If the twigs had been decayed and rigid the line would have parted; as it was, they gave and let him through.

Tigger transferred the rod to his left hand and plunged in, swimming with his right hand and kicking with his legs. The icy shock made him gasp, but the next moment he was back again on firm ground, with the fish running on round the island.

There was a brightness now in the east. Dawn was coming, visibility was improving every minute. Pickle Barrel raced on and then swung out into mid water. Tigger was still connected. The fish tried diving once more but the pressure was still there, maddening and insupportable. He swung his great head round and with a powerful sweep of his tail he hoisted himself into the air like a leaping salmon; fear seemed to give him wings.

For Tigger on the island bank, both hands to the rod and silver drops running down the line, there was visible, for the first time, the true proportions of his opponent.

The mailed golden form broke surface and surged upwards as far as the ventral fins, then fell backwards with a splash which sounded all over the pond. Tigger was too far off to see the connecting line and thought he had jumped free. The spectacle of that enormous battling fish leaping upwards in the dawn light was awe-inspiring. The line was still racing, it was still paying out. Then the rod point ceased to nod, the line became quite immovable. It was as though Tigger had hooked a block of stone.

"This is it," he thought, "this is where I lose him."

Pickle Barrel had gone under the handle of a sunken pram. This had been pushed into the lake some years before by two mischievous boys. It had travelled thirty yards before sinking in a stream of bubbles, in six feet of water and three of mud.

CHAPTER SIX

Weeded

Pickle Barrel lay motionless, resting his pale armoured belly on the mud. The line stretched from his mouth up at an angle to the pram handle, and then on, upwards, through the thick water. His gills moved in and out, gently, like a pair of bellows. His round elephant's eye gazed into nothingness. He only had to go on and turn right or left and the line would have parted like cotton on the immovable pram handle, for the wheels were fast in the clay. But, his fish brain said, 'lie still'.

Up on the bank of the island the boy sat with the rod arched over, the line going straight down at an angle into the pond. "I'll never get him now," he thought. He visualised what might have been his prize, stuffed in a glass case with rushes at the back, like the one he'd seen in the Castle Museum, though his fish would be much larger. It would have had a neat little brass plate at the foot, 'CAUGHT BY T. THOMAS,

JULY 25 1966'. And then the weight (what would that have been? Sixty pounds perhaps, who knows?) He tightened on the line once more, but it was dead. The rod was without life too.

In the corner of Pickle Barrel's muscular mouth the number two forged hook was a little less secure. The continuous strain had weakened the hold, even the bend of the hook was a little more straight, yet over one hundred yards of transparent man-made fibre was still unbroken.

The great fish lay passive, like a resting heavy-weight boxer. He was gathering his strength and was still aware that he had not won free. Little rudd and roach were darting about his looming bulk, goggling with inquisitive ruby eyes, and up above, in that separate world, the summer dawn had truly arrived. A wood pigeon came to the black poplar and cooed, and soon a collared dove came and cooed its own distinctive coo, from one of the chestnuts. It had a mate sitting on eggs down in the thickets, but they would soon be found by the rats.

The swans out on the lake were no longer sleeping. They began to cruise up towards the island. They could see the figure of the boy in the shadow of the bushes and were inquisitive. The cob fluffed out his wings like the petals of a water-lily.

It could not be so long now before Tom's arrival at the boats. Not only Tom. There was Ju Jones the park keeper, a fierce little man with a wary face and a nose like Mr Punches', who always seemed in a bad temper. And no wonder! For years he had waged war on mischievous boys of all ages. If he spotted anyone on the island there would be a rumpus at once. Yet, what was Tigger to do? Cut the line? Never! What would

Hoppy do under these circumstances? Certainly he would never give up any chance of getting Pickle Barrel.

His problem was solved in a curious way. The two swans, the cob in front, and the pen behind, came steadily round the island and bore up directly for Tigger's line. One kick of those sturdy black paddles would cause havoc. They must be stopped but he had no 'catty' like Hoppy's!

His left hand desperately explored the shore of the island by his feet whilst he kept his eye upon the line and the oncoming birds. Luckily his groping fingers encountered a round stone. Holding the rod in his left hand, he threw it. It was a good shot. It landed in a fount of spray just in front of the cob, who back-pedalled, making rude guttural remarks. Bombardments by boys were of common occurrence and at times could be painful. So with arched neck and an expression of outraged dignity, he pushed away, with his wife at his tail.

The stone that Tigger threw so accurately wavered down in a string of bubbles not a foot in front of the round head of Pickle Barrel, resting under the pram handle.

The fish was startled. He swung about and came back under the handle. Had he gone an inch to the right he would have taken the line round the unyielding metal and so broken his tether for good.

The line now began to move swiftly to the right. Once more, to Tigger's great excitement (and renewed hope) the rod became alive, the tip rocking and nodding as he felt the direct, unencumbered, pressure on the fish.

Refreshed with his rest, Pickle Barrel made a spectacular charge down his own channel, and Tigger, weary with lack of sleep, and uncomfortable now in his wet clothes, had no choice but to follow; the same stumbling scramble along the shore of the island.

There was a bed of water-daisy exactly opposite where Tigger had hidden the raft. It was some thirty yards out in the pond and Pickle Barrel's next manoeuvre was to charge straight into this. He went in like a rabbit into its burrow. As he drove forwards with side thrusts of his lobed tail, the clinging tendrils of the weeds enfolded him. Soon, with his struggles, he became the centre of a large cocoon of weed which added considerably to his own weight.

Again the line became immovable, though perhaps not so unyielding as when it was round the pram handle. Nothing Tigger could do stirred the fish, who simply squirmed all the more and gathered to himself more weed.

Tigger, was now near to despair. From time to time the carp stirred within its weed cocoon, and shreds of water-daisy and sheaves of silver bubbles arose, which showed that there was still hope, and that the hook hold was still secure. Had the water been shallower Tigger could have waded out, but it was five feet deep, without counting the mud. There was only one thing for it, *the raft!* This was drawn up under the bushes behind him. If only Pickle Barrel would give him time it might be possible to launch it, get aboard, and get out to the fish where some work with the net handle might get him on the run once more. Was it worth the gamble?

Stealthily he laid down the rod on the ivy leaves. For a moment he watched the line. It still drooped without movement.

Quickly he ran up the bank and dragged the raft down to the water's edge and launched it. He scrambled aboard, picking up the rod in his left hand, praying that the fish was still on. Too late, he remembered the net, but he had the paddle which might do as well for dislodging the fish. With the rod in his left hand, and paddling gently with his right, he advanced on the weed bed. Down in the dense jungle, four feet under, Pickle Barrel sensed the approach of the raft. The shadow of it came slowly overhead like an avenging cloud. Pickle Barrel bolted. The line cut the weeds as a wire cuts cheese. Away went fish, raft, and boy.

Now began a voyage, leisurely it is true, but nevertheless a tour of the pond with Pickle Barrel towing the sledge instead of a sledge dog!

It was almost as if Tigger had a silent outboard engine on the back. Looking behind him for a moment he saw quite a wake in the water, a wake in which small scraps of weed came bobbing to the surface.

Five feet down now in the murky water Pickle Barrel bored doggedly onwards, one green streamer of weed trailing like a banner on the line, which was now chafing his armoured sides where the overlapping scales were dovetailed in, each bigger than a half-crown piece. And the hook hold, which so far had stood so great a strain, was gradually beginning to weaken further.

Did Tigger but know it, disaster was only just round the corner of the island!

CHAPTER SEVEN

Hoppy to the Rescue

The battle between boy and fish now entered what was perhaps its climax.

As Tigger was no longer on firm ground but on a movable, towable object, the stresses and strains he could exert on his adversary were somewhat equalled out. If he reeled in he only drew the raft more swiftly through the water, and then, with his line slackening, the fish went charging on again.

All at once the carp did a complete turn. He rushed right under the raft, bumping the cans with his broad back. It was the first time Tigger had seen the fish at close quarters, and it seemed to him then, that he could never pull so vast a creature out of this pond.

The rod point was hard down on the wood now and bending, bending. The next moment Tigger felt the joint break, about halfway down.

Things happened quickly then. The raft tilted; Tigger took a dive into six feet of weedy water. The raft, thrust onwards by the impetus, voyaged towards the shore some fifty feet distant, followed by the paddle. The rod slid away on its own, towed by Pickle Barrel, with Tigger in threshing pursuit. He had surfaced, shaking his head to get the water from his hair and ears, just in time to see the rod vanish round the island. Then he was into the weeds and in real peril.

If he had lost his head and panicked he would have drowned. The weed tendrils seemed to come up like fiendish fingers and grasp him round his sturdy legs which were red with cold.

Now, though Tigger had learnt to swim, and swim well, and had no fear whatsoever of water, he had never realised the hideous way in which weeds can trap a swimmer. The more he thrust out with legs and arms, the more the slimy green tendrils wrapped themselves around him like the arms of an octopus, or the threads of a spider's web. He did the wisest thing, he turned over on his back and lay still.

Though he did not know it, only two years before, a boy had drowned in the park lake. He had ignored the warning notice, he had swum out beyond the boom towards the island, and had panicked in the weed. Before Tom could reach him with the boat he was dead, and when they pulled him out he was completely enmeshed in a great shroud of weed from head to feet, just as the weed had formed around the fish.

Even though Tigger now lay motionless on his back he felt as if he were bound hand and foot. But, by careful wriggling and pulling at the tendrils, he at last managed to win free. Luckily the island was not more than ten yards away. He

scrambled ashore, completely exhausted, and very frightened. He lay among the ivy leaves with his chest heaving, coughing up water, and wishing he had never come fishing at all.

After a rest he at last felt his strength returning, and then he thought what he had better do.

He walked across the island by the swan's house and looked along the lake for any signs of the rod. Pillars of mist were smoking from the water, uncannily like ghostly figures, for they moved along gently before the breeze of morning. But though he looked until his eyes ached he could see no trace of the rod anywhere. Pickle Barrel must have taken it down with him to the bottom of the pond. What a pity that this great adventure should have ended like this!

Tigger felt he had just about had enough. He was cold and wet through, and his teeth were chattering. At that moment all he wanted was to get ashore, go home, and get to bed. The raft would have to stay where it was, and anyway, he could not bother to fish up the pram wheels and tow the contraption up the park. It was fully light now and traffic was stirring. Soon Tom would be coming.

"That's what I must do," he said to himself, "swim ashore and get away," but he had had enough of weeds and must choose his route with care.

Then, in a moment, the whole situation was changed dramatically. Down across the park came a hobbling figure. *Hoppy!* There was no question now of running home. Hoppy would think of the best way out of their troubles!

Tigger waved wildly. Hoppy waved back, and stood for a moment staring in astonishment at the raft which had drifted in against the rushes, and a short distance along the bank he saw the paddle.

Tigger watched anxiously as his friend retrieved this and clambered aboard the raft. He came paddling across, grinning hugely. Tigger helped him ashore.

"Thought I'd find you on the island," said Hoppy, breathlessly, "but how come the raft and paddle were by the bank?"

"I'll tell you everything in a moment," said Tigger, "but first hadn't we better hide the raft?"

"Sure, let's pull it up among the bushes. It's late enough now, by golly it is, and we shall have to look slippy. Where's the rod?"

That dreaded question! Tigger had been expecting it. For a moment he dare not look at his friend. "The rod's gone, Hoppy, Pickle Barrel went off with it."

Across the park came a hobbling figure.

"*Went off with it?* What do you mean, Tigger?" Hoppy sounded incredulous. And so the whole story had to be told. The hooking of Pickle Barrel, the long, stern battle in the darkness, his peril in the weeds, and finally, the towing of the raft and the loss of the rod.

"Gosh!" exclaimed Hoppy, after he had digested the news. "Dad won't be too bucked about losing his rod and reel, to say nothing of the line. But you had a good try, and we might get the rod yet. What a fish he must be to tow you in the boat like that. Sounds a real fisherman's yarn! Bet Dad won't swallow it!

Well, we'd better get cracking and try and find the rod. If we can't see it from the island, you, or I, will go out in the raft, but time's running out on us, Tigger, Tom'll be here any time. I couldn't get back before. That bobby was real nasty, made me take him back home and he had to talk with Dad. Dad was wild and packed me off to bed, but he didn't mind really, he's a good sport is Dad. Used to fish all night for eels when he was a nipper."

"Right," Tigger said, "let's launch the raft and I'll take a look over by the reeds at the far end."

"You won't," whispered Hoppy, laying a hand on his arm. "Look who's coming along the bank! Down you get and don't move. He can't see us under these bushes."

Tigger looked across the misty water. It was Tom, followed by his little dog. He went along to the boat station. They saw him go into his little hut.

"What do we do now, Hoppy?"

"Do? Stay here of course, stay all day till Tom goes home, and then we'll find the rod. Where's the food bag?"

BOATS
ONDITIONS
OF
HIRE

CHAPTER EIGHT

The Long Day

The boys lay flat on their stomachs under the box bushes. The food bag was between them. Their jaws were working. It was lucky that Hoppy had packed plenty of provisions, enough for both of them (but not enough for Tigger, who had had a lot of exercise, one way or another, including several cold swims).

They could see Tom unlocking the boats and fetching paddles from his hut in readiness for the clients who would soon be arriving in droves. Once or twice the boys saw him pause and look fixedly at the island as though he had seen some suspicious movement, as if he knew there was someone there.

The sun was well up now, over the trees beyond the boat station, and the big chestnuts, which had seemed so forbidding in the dark, were now mounds of misty, silvery green with blue shadows. There was every prospect of another hot day.

Tigger's clothes had now dried. After his breakfast he felt a new man, and ready for anything, but they had to be careful and keep well out of sight, for one never knew where Ju Jones, the park keeper, was prowling around, and the boys knew he carried field-glasses in his pocket so as to spot delinquents, so they had to keep a watch all round them.

"Pass the pop bottle, Tigger," said Hoppy, stretching himself at full length on the ground ivy. He took a long gulp and handed it back. "What about your dad, won't he be wondering what's happened to you?"

"He won't bother. I left him a note in the kitchen to say I was going fishing, so when he came back this morning he wouldn't wonder where I was. Besides, he knows I go with you, and will be fishing till late."

"Looks as if we're here till dark anyway," Hoppy said, "we can't do anything till Tom goes. Still, I don't mind, but we must lie low. If Tom caught us here there'd be no more fishing for me, and we haven't finished with Pickle Barrel yet, not by a long chalk. If we don't find the rod I'll tell Tom to keep a look-out, I can tell him the fish went off with it, see. And there's another thing, Tigger, we don't want to lose the raft. It's a good thing I sunk the pram wheels when I saw the Bobby coming. I saw him before he saw me, that was lucky." "What shall we do when Tom goes?" asked Tigger, munching the last sandwich and wishing there were more.

"We'll launch the raft and one of us, you or me, it don't matter which, will take a row round the lake. I've a notion Pickle Barrel may have gone up the top end where the reeds are. He wouldn't get far, not towing the rod. Once round those lilies he'd break the cast, see, and the rod would come to the top, if he ever took it under, which I doubt. Lucky the reel wasn't a metal one or it might have sunk for good. As it is, there's a chance we'll get it back, and Dad can splice the top joint, easily."

"What say we have a spy on the other side of the island, Hoppy, and I'll show you the swans' house?" Tigger suggested.

"Good idea, let's go, but go on all fours," said Hoppy. Tigger set off, with Hoppy close behind. His iron leg kept catching in the twigs and weeds which made progress slow, but when they reached the far side of the bushes and peered out over the pond towards the shallow end they could see nothing but moorhens pecking about among the flat lily leaves.

"What say I climb a tree?" suggested Tigger, "I'd see better from a higher level."

"Don't be daft! Tom or Ju would spot you in a minute and then where would we be? They'd bring out the boat in no time and we'd be finished. Where's that swans' house you were talking about?"

Tigger, followed by Hoppy, crawled back under the bushes until they came to the clearing. The swan's house had been erected at the same time that the lake was made by the council, who thought a pair of swans would add dignity to the park. It was now in a tumble-down state, with the roof partly fallen in. But it still served as some sort of shelter, as was evident by the number of swans' feathers which lay around, and the piles of droppings.

As the boys entered on all fours a wren flew out and nearly hit Tigger in the face. They found its leaf nest, with an entrance at the side, up in one corner on a cross beam. It was full of hot, pulsing young.

"If we put a window in, and a door, it would make a fine

camping hut," said Hoppy, gazing round appreciatively at the cobwebby interior.

"I'll say, and we could fish for Pickle Barrel whenever we liked."

"Yes, and we'd have an air-gun and shoot moorhens. They make good eating, so my dad says, but they're devils to pluck, so much black wool, even singeing won't get it off."

"Dad was a great one for camping and hunting when he was a boy. Still is. Reckon I get it from him. What about your mum, what was she like, Hoppy?"

"O, I don't know. I can't remember her, and Dad don't talk about her. Anyway, having a woman in the house might have made a difference to my fishing and that. They're terrors for fussing, judging from the woman Dad gets in to clean us up sometimes."

Tigger nodded. "You're right there, Hoppy. They do fuss no end, but all the same I miss my mum. I'll be glad when she's back."

Hoppy rolled over on his stomach, frowning, and chewing a grass stem. It was the first time Tigger had seen his friend looking solemn. He sensed that he had better change the subject.

"Cor, Hoppy, I wish I'd got Pickle Barrel last night. You've no idea what a fish he is, he'd have looked fabulous stuffed."

"We'll have him, we'll have him yet, you see. Gosh, Tigger, when I grow up I'm going to live on an island, with perhaps a drawbridge which I can take up when I don't want anybody to come."

"You mean a moat, like what they had round the old castles?"

"Yes, that's it, Tigger. And I'd have lots of Pickle Barrels swimming round, and other fish, and I'd shoot ducks and that. Gosh, it would be fun! I'd ask you, Tigger, of course, but don't know about any of the other chaps I know. They're not keen on fishing, anyway . . . Hullo, what's old Tom up to?"

Hoppy was peering through the bushes. They could just see the boat station, busy now with children, through a gap in the box leaves.

Tom was launching his row boat, a long, varnished affair of antique design.

"Perhaps one of the kids has fallen in," Tigger suggested, hopefully, trying to peer under Hoppy's arm.

"No, it's not that. Goodness! He's coming past the boom! I'll bet he's seen us on the island. We'll have to hide."

But Tom was not heading for the island. He had only rowed a few strokes and was now looking over his shoulder at something in the pond. Then he stood up in the boat, shading his eyes with his left hand. All the children in the pleasure section had ceased to lark about and were watching him.

"Perhaps one of the kids has lost a ball or something," suggested Tigger.

Tom began to row again.

"O Lord! He's coming this way. If he comes any nearer we'll have to hide in the swans' house and trust to luck."

"If he suspects we're on the island he's sure to look in there," said Tigger sensibly. "We'd be better if we tucked ourselves in the box bushes. What's he doing now, Hoppy?"

"He's standing up again, he's got his oar ready. Reckon you must be right, one of the kids has lost something, ball most likely, or a toy boat. Wait, a minute. No! He's putting his oar in the water trying to hook something. I'll bet it's the rod, Tigger, you have a look."

Tom began to row again.

Tigger pushed his face farther through the thick, hard little leaves. "You're right, it *is* the rod, I can see it moving!"

"Pickle Barrel's still on then!" gasped Hoppy, "Anyway, that's hopeful, we'll get the rod back. Old Tom'll never land him, he don't know anything about fishing."

Tom was certainly having some bother trying to reach the rod. Eventually he appeared to abandon the oar and was reaching over the bow of the boat trying to grab it.

"If old Tom falls in I'd have to fish him out," said Tigger, peering through the thick leaves. "That would be a nice thing, wouldn't it!"

"Here, let's have a look," said Hoppy, pulling his friend away, "what's he doing now?"

"He hasn't got it. Reckon Pickle Barrel's dived with it. There's no weeds there. Tom's looking real mystified. He's getting nearer the island too. O Lord! He's rowing now. He's given up trying to get the rod, he's coming this way. Quick! Let's get under the bushes!"

The boys pushed right under a thicket of bushes which came right down to the ground, and lay flat on their stomachs.

"Make sure your feet don't show," whispered Hoppy, glancing down to make sure his leg iron did not show. "He won't see us if we lie still. Lucky he hasn't got his dog with him. *Hisst!* I can hear the oars!"

The boys lay very still, holding their breaths. They heard the 'tunk tunk' of the oars cease. For some moments all was quiet.

"Perhaps he won't bother to land," whispered Tigger in Hoppy's ear. "Reckon now he's lost the rod he's just coming over to see everything's OK."

They heard no further sounds, but the children were now making a racket up by the boats.

"Hark to them! Tom won't leave those kids long by themselves," whispered Hoppy. *"Hisst!* He's landing! "

They heard sticks cracking on the island. The sound of feet came nearer. From where they lay they could see the swans' house, which was not more than ten yards distant. Soon Tom's wellingtons appeared, the rest of him was obscured by the bushes.

"O Lordy!" breathed Hoppy, "bet he'll spot our food bag. He'll spot the raft too if he goes over to the other side of the island."

Tom's boots vanished behind the swans' house; they heard him muttering to himself.

"If he goes much farther he'll see the bait can and if he finds the raft and landing net we've had it," Tigger whispered.

Just then a regular uproar started from the pleasure boats. The children, realising Tom was absent, and that Ju Jones was nowhere to be seen, were really letting themselves go. Now that Tom was not visible the noise was indescribable. It was the salvation of the two boys on the island.

The wellingtons appeared once more from behind the swans' house and thumped away at a run to where the boat was moored. A moment or two later they heard the cluck of oars, and Tom's loud bellowing, like that of an angry bull, echoed across the pond. Hoppy peered through the bushes once more.

"It's all right, Tigger, Tom's going back past the boom. Reckon we had a narrow shave. What a mercy he landed where he did, down that far end! I don't think he found anything suspicious. The food bag? No, I remember now I put that in the corner of the swans' house, and he wouldn't go right in, he's too big anyway."

"Phew! I'm glad that's over," said Tigger. "Fancy old Pickle Barrel still being on like that! We've got a lively chance of getting the rod I reckon. Tom must have spotted it from his boathouse, or Ju Jones with his field-glasses saw it and told Tom."

Hoppy nodded. "Anyway, I don't reckon he'll come back, he can't be away from those kids for long. He's strict is Tom, and he won't stand any nonsense. Still, we'll keep a look-out, and just hope he doesn't have another search. Reckon he'll be off home when the kids go. He'll want his supper, see, so he won't bother about an old rod."

The shouts and cries of the children up by the boats sounded across the water. A bumbling aeroplane went over. Tigger rolled on his back and looked up into the intricate ceiling of black poplar leaves which filled the whole sky. The slight summer breeze was playing with them, making each silvery leaf wag, and they made a dreamy sound, that mingled with the crying of babies, distant shouts, and the barking of dogs. All the noonday sounds of the park seemed to blend and become blurred and faint. Tigger was very, very tired!

* * *

When he awoke he could not recognise his surroundings. He sat up and looked about him with astonishment. Then he remembered. He rubbed his eyes. Goodness! He must have slept a long time! The sun had gone right round the sky and was now setting over the spire of St Michael's church. There was no sign of Hoppy, but the food bag was outside the swans' house with an apple in it. Hoppy had evidently eaten the other. He realised he was fearfully hungry. He munched the apple and then set off to look for his friend. He had not gone far when he thought he smelt the faint tang of woodsmoke, mingled with the delicious smell of frying fish.

Following his nose like a pointer after game he found Hoppy busy over a fire of holly twigs. On the pile of red embers was the can which had held the bread bait. Steam was rising from it, and it made a bubbling noise. Hoppy heard Tigger push through the bushes. He grinned over his shoulder.

"You've had a long kip haven't you? I've just heard St Michael's clock strike nine. Tom's gone home long ago, didn't come out in the boat again, either, thank goodness."

"What on earth have you got in that can, Hoppy?"

"Eels. Like them?"

"You bet! Dad and I love them, but Mum won't have them in the house."

"I set two eel lines while you were asleep, Tigger. Found some whacking big worms under a stone by the swans' house while you were snoring your head off. They're just about stewed, I guess."

He pushed a stick under the handle of the tin and tipped it sideways to spill out the water. Tigger saw two small eels about a foot long, dark olive green in colour. To grown-ups they would have appeared most repulsive, but not to the boys. Hoppy cut them into sections with his scout knife and then easily pulled off the green skin. Inside, the steaming white boneless flesh, slightly veined, was delicious, just like crab meat.

"Had a job landing them without anyone seeing," said

Hoppy with his mouth full, "they threshed about like snakes. Lucky Ju Jones wasn't around, and that I caught them this side of the island. I saw Tom go home soon after seven. There's still folk about in the park, but we'll get the raft out soon and have a hunt around."

"Wonder nobody noticed the smoke of your fire, though, Hoppy."

"Holly twigs, little ones, that's the secret, Tigger. They don't make much smoke, see, not if you build the fire up careful, and don't put too many sticks on at a time. You go and have a spy, Tigger, and see if the coast's clear yet."

Tigger crawled away through the bushes to where they had hidden the raft. In the west, over the town, there was a salmon pink sky. Lights were beginning to shine from the houses. There was a man, a boy, and a dog romping about at the top of the park; nobody else. They were too far away to notice anything, and the dusk was gathering among the trees like a fog. He was just about to return to Hoppy with his report when a most amazing thing happened. Out of the corner of his eye he saw something moving in the water, right in the middle of Pickle Barrel's swim. It was the missing rod!

It was moving stealthily along, towards him, in jerks. Now and again it stopped altogether, and the rod top, where it had been fractured, jigged a little, sending ripples outwards to the bank.

For a moment Tigger watched it, unbelieving. It was uncanny to see that rod moving so furtively on its own. He was so excited he called out at once, "Hoppy, come here!"

Hoppy came pushing through the undergrowth, his mouth full of eel. "Whatever's the matter? Don't holler like that, you'll . . . " He stopped in mid sentence.

Tigger was pointing at the rod.
There was a moment's pause.
"Grab it, Tigger, Grab it! *Pickle Barrel's still on!"*

CHAPTER NINE

The End of the Affair

Tigger leapt down the bank. He put his foot on a chestnut root. Hoppy took his left hand, and he leaned outwards with the landing net. The rod was travelling slowly parallel to the shore, and was not hard to catch. Tigger got the net ring in front of the big reel and lifted. The next moment he had grabbed the handle and was back on the bank.

"Let's have it, Tigger."

Hoppy gripped the handle triumphantly. He tightened on the line. The top joint hung down like a signal but the line, by some miracle, was still free and had not fouled the rings. Hoppy felt an odd weight on the line, which was trailing weed, but after a moment it came free and he was in direct contact. Pickle Barrel, some thirty yards off down the channel, did not realise what was happening until Hoppy tightened on him. Then he was away out into the lake, sending a bow wave on either side, like a destroyer going into action. Hoppy's face was a study, if only Tigger could have seen it in that dusky place under the trees. The huge ears were twitching backwards and his expression was that of the primitive hunter who has met a worthy opponent.

Like Tigger, hours before, he thrilled to the feel of this monster battling out there in the darkness, but he had more experience in playing a fish. He was more ruthless with the reel, and gave Pickle Barrel short shrift.

The carp shook his huge head from side to side like a dog worries a rat. The hateful tether held.

"Lord, I can't hold him," Hoppy grunted, "pulls like a horse." His face was crimson with excitement, his ears moving.

The carp swung away right-handed now, but Hoppy really gave him the butt in a way that Tigger would never have dared to do, and the fish came round in a great sizzling arc. Hoppy had a tight line on him all the time. The line was chafing again on his scales, like harness rubbing the flanks of a horse.

Hoppy found it extremely difficult to know exactly where the fish was in the pond. The line stretched out into the gloom, but whether it was to left, right, dead ahead, it was impossible to see. This gave him a feeling of helplessness. Then the line suddenly slackened.

"He's off I think," Hoppy muttered miserably. He reeled in and the broken rod joint did not help matters. Then, to his amazement, there was a terrific boil directly under his feet, where brambles bowed over into the water. A big tail broke surface and slapped down like the rudder of a beaver.

"Get the net," gasped Hoppy, still frantically taking in the slack line.

Pickle Barrel had made a fatal mistake. Like the fabled ostrich, he had buried his head in a hole, right under the bank, quite ignorant of the fact that part of his long dorsal fin and most of his tail lobes were flapping wildly in full view.

A hunted fish, whether it is a royal salmon or a humble carp, will frequently take refuge in a hole under a bank. A smaller fish might have got away with it, but Pickle Barrel was handicapped by his size.

"Here, Tigger, take the rod, quick! If he makes a dash for it let him have line, and keep the rod point down. I'm going to have a shot at netting him."

Hoppy knelt on the bank, his knees shaking with excitement. He placed the big net ring behind the tail which was lashing the brambles. Though it was a large-sized net, in which Hoppy's dad had landed a twenty-pound Fenland pike, it seemed far too small to encompass this vast fish, but there was no alternative. He held the shaft upright with both hands and pressed it close into the brambles, over the waving tail. Leaning over he could see a broad netted back. The head and shoulders were completely hidden under the overhang and undergrowth.

Pickle Barrel felt the net touch his tail. Something pushed in behind him. He thought it was a hunting otter. With a great thrusting heave he turned around. The line caught on the sharp spine at the front of his dorsal fin. It was cut like cotton on a razor's edge. He was free.

With a terrific charge he came out of the hole. He went head first into the net. He went with such force he almost toppled Hoppy in, and as for Tigger, when the line went, he fell backwards into the brambles. For a moment there was chaos.

Hoppy was aware of only one thing. He must hold on to the net at all costs. There was a mighty threshing of white water which drenched him, the net handle jumped in his hand, then Tigger was down the bank waist deep, beside him. Together they heaved. Hoppy managed to grab the net in both hands and clutch the thick part of Pickle Barrel's tail through the meshes of the net. Tigger pulled on the shaft.

With a terrific heave, both together, they managed to haul net and fish up the bank. It was like carrying a sucking pig in a pig net. It took their united strength. Then they turned the net over. The huge mailed form rolled, gasping, on the ground ivy.

There, on the shiny leaves he heaved and flapped, his funnel-shaped mouth opening and shutting, his small intelligent eyes rolled downwards in an expression of horror.

"O, what a fish!" gasped Hoppy, when he could get his breath. "*What a fish.* Won't Dad sit up when he sees this! Let's measure him. Hold him steady." He pulled from his pocket a folding angler's rule.

"Three-foot-five from nose to tail," Hoppy announced in triumph. Then he measured the girth, "Thirty-five inches round. That beats the record, easy, Tigger. We'll be famous! He'll go well over fifty, but we can't weigh him until we get him home."

Pickle Barrel continued to stare downwards, cross-eyed. The massive barrel of a frame gave a convulsive jump on the leaves. His hold on life was going, he could not save it.

"We'll have him set up, Tigger, by gum we will!" said Hoppy, gloating. "Won't he look smashing in a glass case? He's really your fish, Tigger, you hooked him, and played him all last night. He's yours really. Hold him there, I'll fetch him

He heaved with all his strength.

a fourpenny one with the net handle. Wait till I unscrew it."

Hoppy knelt in the shadow and gripped the net shaft. The slime from Pickle Barrel's scales made the metal slippery.

Tigger had both hands resting on the cold scales. He stared down at the distressed face of this monstrous fish and felt a sudden wave of remorse and pity. Why should Pickle Barrel die just because he was big?

He glanced round over his shoulder. Hoppy was bent over the net trying to unscrew it, red in the face, his tongue between his teeth in frantic concentration. Tigger placed both hands under the massive cold body with its overlapping armour. He heaved with all his strength.

Pickle Barrel rolled, slowly at first, then gathering speed, with leaves and grit sticking to his scales, till he hit the water with a mighty splash.

For a moment his submerging dorsal fin moved sluggishly forward towards the open water.

One more roll, a brief glimpse. He was gone!

Hoppy never saw it happen. He was still struggling with the shaft. He heard the sullen, heavy plunge and his head jerked up, apprehensively.

"What the hell was that?"

Tigger, kneeling on the bank, stared unseeing at the subsiding ripples. He knew.